Tarantulas

Tarantulas

Peter Murray

THE CHILD'S WORLD®

Published in the United States of America by The Child's World®
PO Box 326
Chanhassen, MN 55317-0326
800-599-READ
www.childsworld.com

Project Manager Mary Berendes
Editor Katherine Stevenson, Ph.D.
Designer Mary Berendes
**Our sincere thanks to Robert Mitchell, Ph.D.,
for his input and guidance on this book.**

Photo Credits
© Brian Kenney: 16, 19, 23
© J. Mitchell, O.S.F./Animals Animals: 13
© Mitch Diamond/Index Stock Imagery, Inc: 30
© Rhys A. Brigida: 15
© Robert & Linda Mitchell: cover, 9, 10, 20 (both), 24, 26, 29 (both)
© The Image Bank/Gary Vestal: 2
© Willie Holdman/Index Stock Imagery, Inc.: 6

Library of Congress Cataloging-in-Publication Data
Murray, Peter, 1952 Sept. 29–
Tarantulas / by Peter Murray.
p. cm.
ISBN 1-56766-980-8 (lib. bdg. : alk. paper)
1. Tarantulas—Juvenile literature.
[1. Tarantulas. 2. Spiders.] I. Title.
QL458.42.T5 M87 2003
595.4'4—dc21
2001000304

On the cover...

Front cover: This king baboon tarantula lives in Africa.
Page 2: This desert tarantula is walking on a flower in Texas.

Table of Contents

Chapter	Page
Meet the Tarantula!	7
What Are Tarantulas?	8
Are There Different Kinds of Tarantulas?	12
How Do Tarantulas Hunt?	14
How Do Tarantulas Eat?	18
How Are Baby Tarantulas Born?	21
How Do Baby Tarantulas Grow Up?	22
Do Tarantulas Have Enemies?	27
How Do Tarantulas Stay Safe?	28
Do Tarantulas Make Good Pets?	31
Glossary, Index, & Web Sites	32

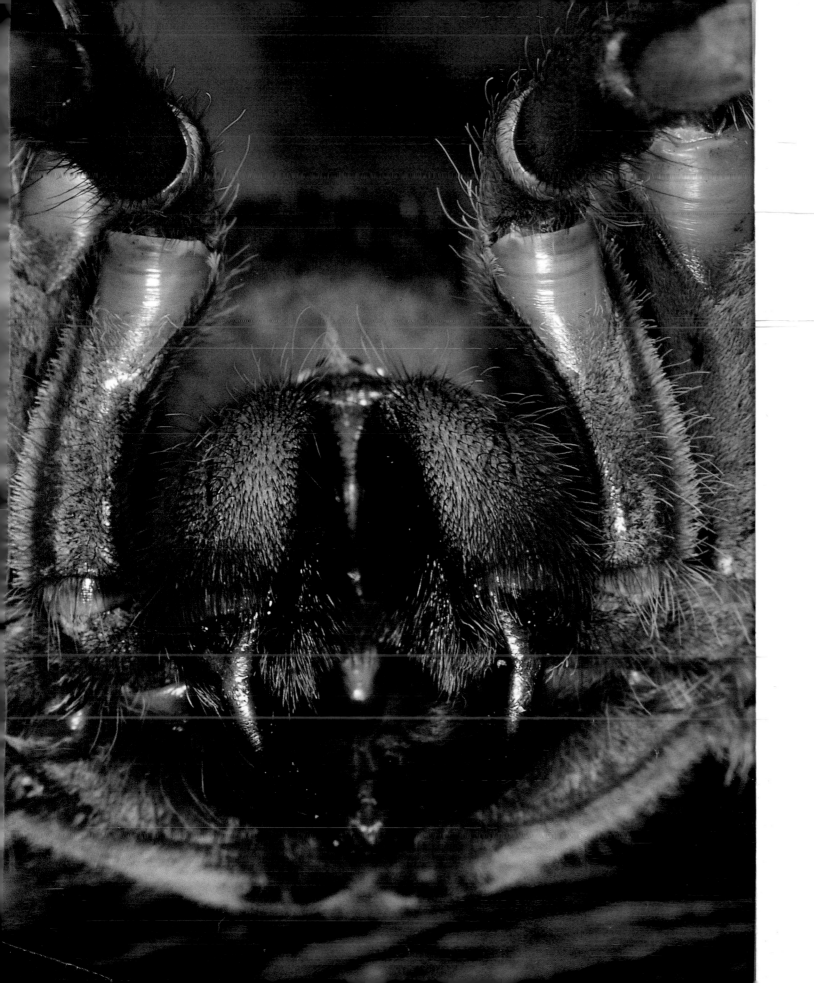

You are walking in the desert, enjoying the warm sunshine, when you see a small hole in the ground. What kind of animal lives there? Could it be a mouse? A lizard? You sit down and wait. After a long, long time you see movement. A hairy leg as long as your little finger reaches out of the hole. Another leg reaches out, and then another, and another! Finally you see eight legs and a fat, fuzzy brown body. What is this strange creature? It's a tarantula!

⇐ This desert tarantula is moving carefully over a bare patch of ground.

What Are Tarantulas?

Tarantulas are spiders. They have eight hairy legs, eight eyes, and a body divided into two areas. The spider's head and chest are in the front area, or **cephalothorax**. The back area, or **abdomen**, is the spider's stomach region.

Like most other spiders, tarantulas can spin silk from their abdomens. But instead of making webs to catch insects, they use the soft silk for lining their nests.

This is a female Mexican bloodleg tarantula. ⇒

Like all spiders, tarantulas make poison called **venom** inside their bodies. The venom squirts out from the tarantula's fangs. This venom is dangerous to insects and other animals the spiders eat. Most of the time, it isn't dangerous to people. Being bitten by most tarantulas is no worse than being stung by a bee—it hurts, but not for long.

⇐ Here you can see the fangs of a king baboon tarantula.

Are There Different Kinds of Tarantulas?

There are more than 800 different kinds, or **species**, of tarantulas. They live in warmer areas of the world, such as Mexico, South America, Africa, India, Australia, and the southwestern United States. Some tarantula species live in holes in the ground, called *burrows*. Others live in trees.

Most tarantulas are small enough to fit in the palm of your hand. But the *goliath birdeating spider*, the largest species, grows as big as a dinner plate! These giant, burrowing tarantulas live only in South America. Unlike most tarantulas, goliath birdeaters eat small birds, bats, frogs, and even snakes! Most tarantulas eat smaller animals such as insects, and sometimes other spiders.

This picture shows a goliath birdeating spider at ⇒ actual size. Hold your hand up to the picture. Would you like this spider crawling on you?

How Do Tarantulas Hunt?

Tarantulas have poor eyesight, so they use feelers called **pedipalps** to tell where they are going. Tarantulas also move very slowly. So how do they catch their dinner? To avoid enemies that might try to eat them, tarantulas do their hunting at night. In the darkness they can move around and hunt for food without being bothered.

This goliath birdeater has found a baby bird to eat. ⇒

Like all spiders, tarantulas can sense tiny movements, or **vibrations**, made by other animals. When a tarantula is hungry, it finds a hiding place. When the spider senses the vibrations of a **prey** animal, it holds very still. With any luck, the prey will walk nearby. If it does, the spider quickly runs toward the prey. Then it lifts the front of its body and pushes its two long fangs into the prey. As the fangs enter the prey's body, the tarantula shoots out its deadly venom. The prey dies, and the tarantula enjoys its meal.

⇐ This cobalt blue birdeater tarantula has found a grasshopper to eat.

How Do Tarantulas Eat?

To eat, the tarantula first shoots special liquids into its prey. The liquids soften the prey's insides and make it easier to eat. Using its fangs and pedipalps, the tarantula presses the prey animal against its mouth. Then it slowly sucks the juices out of the prey.

Sometimes, a prey animal passes by a tarantula that isn't hungry. The spider attacks and kills the prey anyway. Instead of eating it right away, the tarantula wraps the dead prey in silk. Then it drags the prey back to its burrow and saves it for a later meal.

This Colombian brown tarantula is feeding on a grasshopper. ⇒

How Are Baby Tarantulas Born?

For most of the year, tarantulas live by themselves. But each fall, male and female tarantulas get together to mate. Then the male quickly crawls away. If he stays around, the female might try to eat him!

For the next few weeks, the female has a huge appetite. She hunts every day, and her abdomen grows larger. Finally, she spins a thick, flat mat of webbing on the floor of her burrow. Some types of tarantula females lay several hundred eggs on the web. Other types lay less than one hundred. Then the female wraps her eggs into a big white ball of silk called an **egg sac**. The female guards her egg sac for about six weeks. During cool nights, she even covers the ball with her body to keep the eggs warm. Then the eggs hatch, and the baby spiders emerge.

⇐ *Main photo*: This female Costa Rican curlyhair tarantula is laying her eggs.

Small photo: This female Indian ornamental tarantula is guarding her egg sac. 21

How Do Baby Tarantulas Grow Up?

A few days after they hatch, the baby tarantulas leave their mother's burrow and quickly search for hiding places of their own. This is the most dangerous time in a tarantula's life. Many baby tarantulas are eaten by lizards, snakes, birds, and other tarantulas. Those that survive dig burrows, and there they will spend most of their lives. If a tarantula can survive its first few months, it might live for as long as 25 years!

Here you can see baby Brazilian salmon pink tarantulas. ⇒

Instead of having bones on the inside of its body, a tarantula has a hard, shell-like skin called an **exoskeleton**. As the spider grows, the exoskeleton stays the same size. So how can a baby grow into an adult? As the baby grows, it **molts**, or sheds its outgrown exoskeleton. A new exoskeleton is waiting just under the old one.

At first, the new exoskeleton is soft and stretchable. The spider must stay in a safe place for a few days until its new exoskeleton hardens. Once the exoskeleton is hard, the tarantula can move about more safely. A tarantula molts several times during its lifetime. If it loses a leg, the leg slowly grows back during the next few molts!

⇐ This Costa Rican zebra tarantula is molting.
Her old skin is in the lower part of the photo.

Do Tarantulas Have Enemies?

Snakes, birds, and even some lizards think tarantulas are a tasty treat. But one enemy is different from the rest. *Tarantula hawk wasps* use tarantulas as living meals for their babies. The female tarantula hawk wasp lands near a tarantula's burrow and waits. When the spider comes out, the wasp stings it. When it stings, the wasp injects venom into the spider, making the spider unable to move.

The wasp drags the helpless tarantula into a hole. Then she lays an egg on the spider and covers the hole with dirt. A few days later, a wormlike wasp larva hatches from the egg. The hungry larva then feeds on the tarantula—slowly eating it alive!

⇐ Here a tarantula hawk wasp captures a tarantula in Arizona.

How Do Tarantulas Stay Safe?

A tarantula's fangs are long and fierce looking, but they are not the spider's first choice for defense. Instead, a threatened tarantula usually runs and hides. If cornered, a tarantula will rear back and show its long fangs to try to scare its attacker away. This makes the tarantula look bigger and scarier than it really is. Sometimes, a tarantula will even lunge forward to strike with its fangs!

If that doesn't work, some tarantulas have one more defense. They uses their hind legs to break special hairs off their abdomen. These hairs float through the air, often getting into the skin and eyes of the attacker. The hairs are extremely irritating.

Main photo: This male Malayan earth tiger tarantula feels ⇒ threatened. He has raised his front legs to appear larger.

Inset: This female Mexican redknee tarantula has a bare patch where she has kicked off her abdomen hairs.

Do Tarantulas Make Good Pets?

Surprisingly, tarantulas can make very good pets. If you ever get a pet tarantula, you must be very gentle with it. It is not a good idea to let your tarantula crawl on you—not because it might bite, but because it might fall! Tarantulas are easily hurt, and a fall to the floor can kill them.

The best home for a pet tarantula is a **terrarium** with glass sides. The terrarium should have everything the spider would have in the wild. That includes fresh water, live food, and a hiding place. But even if you don't have a tarantula as a pet, you can still appreciate these beautiful spiders!

⟸ This girl is carefully touching a pet tarantula.

Glossary

abdomen (AB-doh-men)
The back area of a spider's body is called its abdomen. The spider's abdomen contains organs that spin silk.

cephalothorax (seh-fuh-loh-THOR-ax)
The front area of a spider's body is called its cephalothorax. A tarantula's cephalothorax contains its eyes, mouth, fangs, and stomach.

egg sac (EGG SAK)
An egg sac is a baglike holder in which some animals place their eggs to keep them safe. Female tarantulas make egg sacs out of silk they produce in their bodies.

exoskeleton (eks-oh-SKEL-eh-tun)
An exoskeleton is a hard outer covering some animals have instead of bones. Tarantulas have an exoskeleton.

molt (MOLT)
When an animal molts, it sheds its outer layer of skin, fur, or feathers. Adult tarantulas molt several times during their lifetime.

pedipalps (PED-ih-palps)
Pedipalps are the leglike feelers a spider has between its jaws and legs. Tarantulas use their pedipalps to eat, grab things, and feel their way around.

prey (PRAY)
Animals that are eaten by other animals are called prey. Insects, lizards, and sometimes other spiders are prey for tarantulas.

species (SPEE-sheez)
A species is a different kind of an animal. There are more than 800 different species of tarantulas.

terrarium (teh-REHR-ee-um)
A terrarium is a container used for raising small animals or plants. Pet tarantulas are best kept in glass terrariums.

venom (VEN-um)
Venom is poison some animals make in their bodies. Tarantulas have a venom that is fairly harmless to people.

vibrations (vy-BRAY-shunz)
Vibrations are small movements. Tarantulas can feel vibrations made by the animals they hunt.

Index

abdomen, 8, 21
appearance, 7, 8, 12, 25
bites from, 11
burrows, 12, 18, 21, 22, 27
cephalothorax, 8
defense, 28
eggs, 21
egg sac, 21
enemies, 22, 27
exoskeleton, 25
eyes, 8
fangs, 11, 17, 18, 28
feeding, 18
food, 12, 14, 17
goliath birdeating spider, 12
growing, 25
hunting, 14, 17
legs, 7
life span, 22
living areas, 7, 12
molting, 25
movement, 14
nests, 8
pedipalps, 14, 18
as pets, 31
prey, 17, 18
silk, 8, 18, 21
special hairs, 28
species, 12
staying safe, 14, 22, 25, 28
tarantula hawk wasp, 27
terrarium, 31
venom, 11, 17
vibrations, 17
young, 21, 22, 25

Web Sites

Visit our homepage for lots of links about tarantulas!

http://www.childsworld.com/links.html

Note to Parents, Teachers, and Librarians:
We routinely verify our Web links to make sure they're safe, active sites—so encourage your readers to check them out!